Oxford Read and Discover

D1579425

Rob Sved

OXFORD

UNIVERSITY PRESS

OXFORD
UNIVERSITY PRESS

Great Clarendon Street, Oxford, OX2 6DP, United Kingdom

Oxford University Press is a department of the University of Oxford. It furthers the University's objective of excellence in research, scholarship, and education by publishing worldwide. Oxford is a registered trade mark of Oxford University Press in the UK and in certain other countries

ISBN: 978 0 19 464629 1

An Audio CD Pack containing this book and a CD is also available, ISBN 978 0 19 464639 0

The CD has a choice of American and British English recordings of the complete text.

An accompanying Activity Book is also available, ISBN 978 0 19 464650 5

Printed in China

This book is printed on paper from certified and well-managed sources.

ACKNOWLEDGEMENTS

Illustrations by: Kelly Kennedy pp.7, 9; Alan Rowe pp.20, 22, 23, 24, 25, 26, 27, 28, 30, 31.

The Publishers would also like to thank the following for their kind permission to reproduce photographs and other copyright material: Getty Images pp.14 (David Haring/Oxford Scientific), 15 (flashlight fish/Norbert Wu/Minden Pictures), 16 (spider/ George Grall/National Geographic), 19 (meercats/Barcroft Media, girl/Jon Ragel/The Image Bank); Naturepl.com pp.3 (duck/Rolf Nussbaumer), 4 (duck/Rolf Nussbaumer), 7 (owl small pupil/John Cancalosi, owl large pupil/Staffan Widstrand), 8 (Marcus Varesvuo), 11 (stalk-eyed fly/Phil Savoie, chameleon/Tony Phelps), 12 (Alex Mustard), 15 (cat/ John Downer), 18 (Hanne & Jens Eriksen); Oxford University Press p.5; Photolibrary pp.3 (monkey/David & Micha Sheldon/F1Online), 4 (gecko/Martin Harvey/Peter Arnold Images), 6 (Nick Garbutt/Oxford Scientific), 9 (David & Micha Sheldon/F1Online), 10 (shark/Norbert Probst/imagebroker. net), 13 (flatfish (top)/Claude Guihard/Bios), 16 (scallop/ Christophe Migeon/Bios), 21 (Nick Garbutt/Oxford Scientific); Science Photo Library pp.3 (tree frog/Martin Shields, fish/ Scubazoo), 10 (tree frog/Martin Shields), 13 (Pygmy sweeper fish (bottom)/Scubazoo), 17 (dragonfly eyes close-up/Claude Nuridsany & Marie Perennou, dragonfly (inset)/Herman Eisenbeiss).

 # Introduction

People and animals see with their eyes. You have two eyes. Some animals have many eyes. Eyes can be little or big, and they can be many colors.

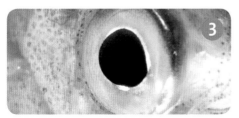

What animals have these eyes? What color are your eyes?

 Now read and discover more about eyes!

A Duck

What do animals do with their eyes? They look for food. The duck looks for food in water.

The gecko has big eyes. It can see well at night. It looks for insects to eat.

A Gecko

A Crab

Eyes help to protect animals from other animals. The crab has two eyes on top of its body. It can see big animals, and then it can run away.

→ Go to page 20 for activities.

2 Parts of an Eye

Let's look at an eye. It has many parts. This is an elephant's eye. The eyelid and the eyelashes protect the eyeball. There are tears in the eye, too. The eyelid opens and closes, and the tears clean the eye.

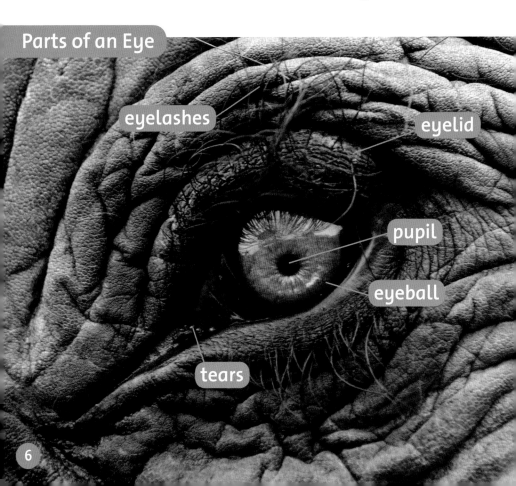

Parts of an Eye

eyelashes

eyelid

pupil

eyeball

tears

little pupil

big pupil

The pupil lets light into the eye. This helps people and animals to see. When there's lots of light, the pupil is little. When there's no light, the pupil is big.

Discover!

People have tears to clean their eyes. People cry tears when they are sad, too!

→ Go to page 21 for activities.

Eyes at the Front

People and many animals have two eyes at the front of their head. This helps them to see things far away.

The hawk can fly fast and it can see very well, too. This helps it to hunt little animals to eat.

A Hawk

A Monkey

The monkey has eyes at the front of its head. It can jump from tree to tree and it doesn't fall.

Discover!

Owls have eyes at the front of their head. Some owls can move their head around and see behind!

→ Go to page 22 for activities.

Eyes at the Sides

Many animals have eyes at the sides of their head. They can see in front and behind.

The frog has eyes at the sides of its head. It can look for insects to eat.

The hammerhead shark has a long, flat head. It has eyes at the sides of its head. When it swims, it can see all around.

A Tree Frog

A Hammerhead Shark

eye

stalk

A Stalk-Eyed Fly

The stalk-eyed fly can see all around, too. It has eyes on two long stalks.

Discover!

The chameleon sees all around very well. One eye moves up, and the other eye moves down!

Go to page 23 for activities.

 # In Water

The seal lives on land and in water.
It has big, round eyes. It can see
very well in water. It hunts fish
to eat.

A Seal

A Flatfish

The flatfish has two eyes on one side of its body. It can lie at the bottom of the ocean and look up.

Discover! Fish live in water, and they don't have eyelids. They don't close their eyes!

Go to page 24 for activities.

6 In the Dark

At night, some animals sleep. Many other animals look for food. The lemur looks for fruit and little animals to eat. It has big eyes with big pupils. It can see very well in the dark.

A Lemur

It's very dark at the bottom of the ocean. The flashlight fish has lights under its eyes. This helps it to look for little fish to eat.

In the dark, cats and dogs have bright eyes. They can see very well. Look at this cat. What color are its eyes?

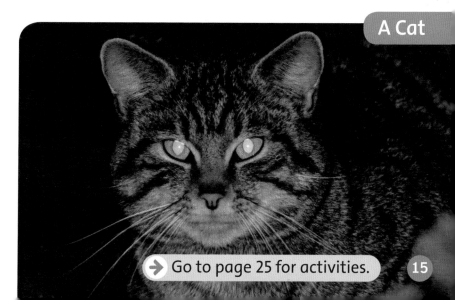

A Cat

Go to page 25 for activities.

15

7 Many Eyes

A Spider

Some animals have many eyes.
Many spiders have six or eight eyes.

The scallop can have more than
50 little eyes! How many of the
eyes can you see here?

A Scallop

eye

Some insects have very many eyes.
Look at this dragonfly. Each eye is
thousands of little eyes together.

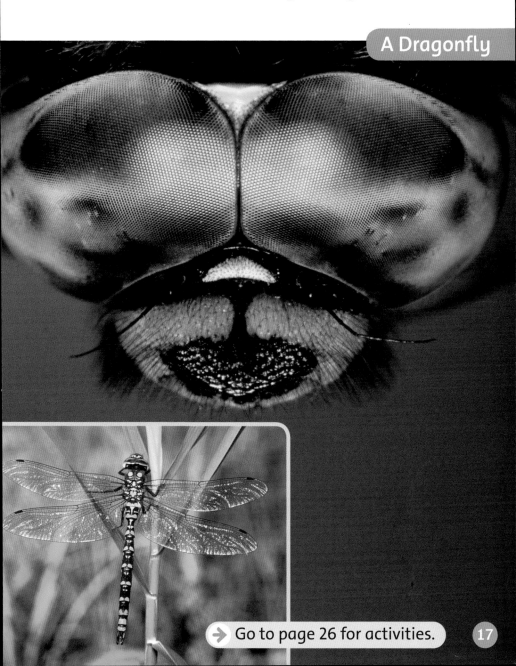

A Dragonfly

Go to page 26 for activities.

Protect Your Eyes

It's important for animals to protect their eyes. In the desert there's a lot of sand. The camel has long eyelashes so the sand doesn't go in its eyes.

Camels

black fur

Meerkats

The meerkat lives in the desert, too. It's sunny and windy there. Its eyelids clean the sand from its eyes. The meerkat has black fur around its eyes. This protects its eyes when it's sunny.

People wear sunglasses when it's very sunny. This protects their eyes. Eyes are important. Remember to protect them!

→ Go to page 27 for activities.

1 Animal Eyes

← Read pages 4–5.

1 Write the words. Then match.

1 b r c a

___crab___

2 k c e g o

_____

3 c t s i s n e

_____

4 c d k u

_____

2 Complete the sentences.

see ~~look~~ top big

1 Animals ___look___ for food with their eyes.

2 The gecko has _____ eyes.

3 The gecko can _____ well at night.

4 The crab has eyes on _____ of its body.

2 Parts of an Eye

← Read pages 6–7.

1 Write the words.

~~eyelashes~~   eyelid   tears   eyeball   pupil

1 *eyelashes*

2 _____

3 _____

4 _____

5 _____

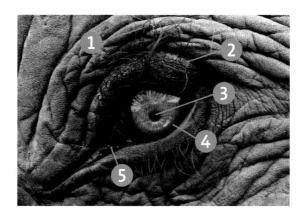

2 Write *true* or *false*.

1 Tears clean the eye.   *true*

2 The pupil doesn't let light into
   the eye.   _____

3 When there's lots of light, the
   pupil is big.   _____

4 People cry when they are sad.   _____

21

③ Eyes at the Front

← Read pages 8–9.

1 Find and write the words.

a	o	w	l	r	g
j	u	m	p	t	k
a	o	h	s	a	t
m	n	h	a	w	k
p	h	u	n	t	u
m	o	n	k	e	y

1 ___hawk___

2 __m_____

3 __h_____   4 __o_____   5 __j_____

2 Match.

1 The hawk can
2 People have eyes
3 The monkey can
4 Some owls can

jump from tree to tree.

turn their head around.

at the front of their head.

fly fast.

④ Eyes at the Sides

← Read pages 10–11.

stalk-eyed fly
hammerhead shark
frog   chameleon

1 Write the words.

1 _____

_____

2 _____

_____

3 _____

4 _____

2 Circle the correct words.

1 The hammerhead shark has a long,
   (flat)/ **round** head.

2 The frog has eyes at the sides of its
   body / **head**.

3 The stalk-eyed fly has eyes on **two** / **four**
   long stalks.

4 The chameleon **can** / **can't** see all around.

5 In Water

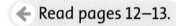 Read pages 12–13.

1 Write *true* or *false*.

1 The seal lives on land and in water. _____

2 The seal hunts insects to eat. _____

3 The flatfish can lie at the bottom
of the ocean. _____

4 Fish have eyelids. _____

2 Find and write the words.

Oceanlandeyesflatfishsealwater

1 _____ 2 _____ 3 _____

4 __ocean__ 5 _____ 6 _____

6 In the Dark

← Read pages 14–15.

1 Complete the sentences.

> pupils   lights   dark   dogs

1 The lemur has big eyes with big _____.

2 At the bottom of the ocean it's very

_____.

3 The flashlight fish has _____ under its eyes.

4 Cats and _____ have bright eyes in the dark.

2 Read and complete the pictures.

1 The lemur has big eyes with big pupils.

2 The flashlight fish has lights under its eyes.

3 In the dark, this cat has yellow eyes.

7 Many Eyes

← Read pages 16–17.

1 Write the words.

scallop   spider   dragonfly

1 _____   2 _____   3 _____

2 Complete the sentences.

six or eight   thousands   more than 50

1 Many spiders have _____ eyes.

2 The scallop has _____ eyes.

3 The dragonfly has _____ of eyes.

3 Find and write the words.

insectsanimalsbigeyeslittlemany

1 _____   3 _____   5 _____

2 _____   4 _____   6 _____

8 Protect Your Eyes

← Read pages 18–19.

1 Write the words.

1 adsn

2 resdet

3 seglsaunss

_____

_____

_____

4 urf

5 dnyiw

6 nusny

_____

_____

_____

2 How do they protect their eyes? Match.

1 people	long eyelashes
2 meerkats	sunglasses
3 camels	fur around the eyes

My Eyes

1   Look in a mirror and draw your eyes.
    Write the parts.

eyeball   eyelashes   pupil   eyelid

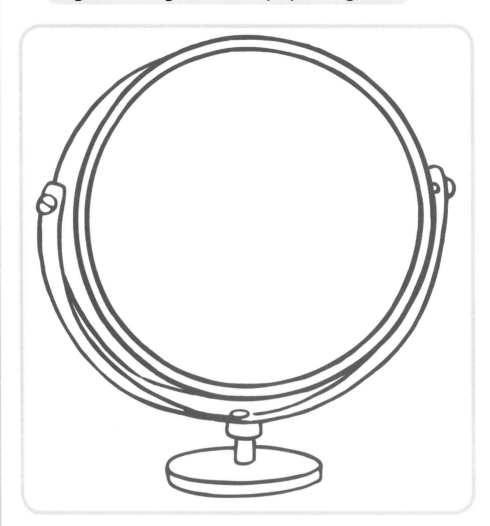

2 **Write about your eyes.**

How many eyes do you have?

I have _____

What color are your eyes?

_____

Are your eyes big or little?

_____

Are your eyes at the front or at the sides?

_____

Can you see in water?

_____

Can you see in the dark?

_____

What protects your eyes?

_____

_____

Picture Dictionary

 animals

 around

 behind

 bottom

 bright

 clean

 cry

 dark

 desert

 down

 fall

 far

 fast

 flat

 food

 front

fruit   hunt   insects   land

light   night   ocean   people

protect   sand   sides   sleep

tears   thousand   top   up

Oxford Read and Discover

Series Editor: Hazel Geatches • CLIL Adviser: John Clegg

Oxford Read and Discover graded readers are at six levels, for students from age 6 and older. They cover many topics within three subject areas, and support English across the curriculum, or Content and Language Integrated Learning (CLIL).

Available for each reader:
• Audio CD Pack (book & audio CD)
• Activity Book

Teaching notes & CLIL guidance: www.oup.com/elt/teacher/readanddiscover

Subject Area / Level	The World of Science & Technology	The Natural World	The World of Arts & Social Studies
1 — 300 headwords	• Eyes • Fruit • Trees • Wheels	• At the Beach • In the Sky • Wild Cats • Young Animals	• Art • Schools
2 — 450 headwords	• Electricity • Plastic • Sunny and Rainy • Your Body	• Camouflage • Earth • Farms • In the Mountains	• Cities • Jobs
3 — 600 headwords	• How We Make Products • Sound and Music • Super Structures • Your Five Senses	• Amazing Minibeasts • Animals in the Air • Life in Rainforests • Wonderful Water	• Festivals Around the World • Free Time Around the World
4 — 750 headwords	• All About Plants • How to Stay Healthy • Machines Then and Now • Why We Recycle	• All About Desert Life • All About Ocean Life • Animals at Night • Incredible Earth	• Animals in Art • Wonders of the Past
5 — 900 headwords	• Materials to Products • Medicine Then and Now • Transportation Then and Now • Wild Weather	• All About Islands • Animal Life Cycles • Exploring Our World • Great Migrations	• Homes Around the World • Our World in Art
6 — 1,050 headwords	• Cells and Microbes • Clothes Then and Now • Incredible Energy • Your Amazing Body	• All About Space • Caring for Our Planet • Earth Then and Now • Wonderful Ecosystems	• Food Around the World • Helping Around the World